Amazon Prime

How to Make the Most Out of the Many Benefits of Amazon Prime Membership

Table Of Contents

Introduction

I want to thank you and congratulate you for downloading the book Amazon Prime: How to Make the Most Out of the Many Benefits of Amazon Prime Membership. You are on your way to becoming a pro at using all the features Amazon Prime has to offer.

This book contains proven steps and strategies on how to truly make the most out of your Prime membership, including borrowing books, streaming media, and getting special member privileges such as fast, free shipping.

Here's an inescapable fact: there are so many benefits of a Prime membership, it is possible to be overwhelmed and not sure exactly what you can do with it. That is where this book comes in, providing an overview of benefits as well as some in-depth how-to instructions to really utilize Amazon Prime.

If you got your Prime membership just to use one feature, you may really miss out on other services that you would love. Amazon Prime is designed to make your life run smoother. You may find yourself surprised at some of the things Amazon Prime can do for you!

It's time for you to become an expert on using Amazon Prime and take advantage of the movies, television shows, music, photo storage, shopping options, books, and more available to you with your membership!

Chapter 1: Is Amazon Prime for Me?

Amazon Prime is not a free service, and you may be wondering if you will get enough use out of it to make it worth the $99/year or the $10.99/month. So what types of people will get the most use out of an Amazon Prime membership?

People who do a lot of online shopping can make their money back pretty quickly. You can shop for nearly anything on Amazon. True, any order of over $49 dollars made up of eligible items ships free even without Prime, but using standard shipping which can take 7-10 business days to arrive. Prime members can have no minimum purchase when buying qualifying items in order to qualify for free 2-day shipping. If you frequently make smaller purchases or want free and fast shipping, you should consider becoming an Amazon Prime member,

Do you prefer watching television shows and movies through streaming services? Amazon has a large library and a comparable price to other services. When you throw in the other features you are getting as a member, Amazon

Prime comes out looking like a better deal. Amazon Video streaming is also available on most devices used by the other services. Amazon Video is the first to offer High Dynamic Range video quality, so if you are a stickler for the best in video and audio experience, an Amazon Prime membership could serve you well.

Want to stream music without interruptions? Amazon Music may not have as large of a library as some of the other streaming services, but as a Prime member, you will not have to listen to ads between songs or be limited to the number of times you can skip a track.

Are you a frequent flyer? If so, and you fly JetBlue, you can stream Prime music and videos for free on your flight. JetBlue has a fleet of Fly-Fi planes that allow you to access your Amazon Prime benefits. You can use your laptop, Android or iOS smartphone, or your Amazon Kindle to help the time and miles fly by.

Chapter 2: Overview of Benefits and Rules

Becoming an Amazon Prime member comes with a wide variety of benefits, as well as some rules and regulations you should be aware of. Let's talk about the perks first.

Shipping

Amazon Prime does not use one shipping carrier exclusively, but instead uses whichever one will get you your item in the time frame you have specified.

Many items on Amazon are available to receive free 2-day shipping in the continental United States. This applies to items sold by Amazon, not through the Amazon Marketplace. If you live in Hawaii, Alaska, or Puerto Rico you will get free 3-7 day shipping instead. It is important to note that the 2-day period starts after the item ships, so if you order something that is currently out of stock you will get it 2 days after they get the item in and ship it to you. Set your default shipping address to see reliable estimates of when your items will arrive. Remember, only business days count when calculating when your item will arrive. Saturday shipping is available on some specially marked items, with prices starting at $7.99 and going up based on weight and size. Release-Date Delivery is an exciting and free shipping option available for qualifying items.

In some larger cities, Amazon Prime members can even get same-day shipping, as long as they select items marked eligible for the service. There is a minimum purchase of $35 for this service and orders generally have to be in by noon or they will be changed to free 1-day shipping. This service is available 7 days a week, with the exception of major holidays and high volume shipping days, such as Black Friday.

If you are not in a great hurry to get your items, you can choose No-Rush Shipping at checkout. If you do this, Amazon will reward you with a promotional credit of some kind. The credit could be for music, videos, Amazon Pantry, or buying an e-book, among other things. You will be told what your specific credit is for when you choose your shipping method at checkout. You will still receive your item within 5 business days. In order to hold on to your credit, do not cancel the No-Rush Shipping or return the item you ordered. Amazon will credit your account as soon as your order ships and even automatically apply it to qualifying purchases!

Prime Video

There are thousands of titles available to stream free for Prime members. Some titles are even available to download to an Amazon Kindle or mobile devices to view offline. The catalog of movies and T.V. shows changes frequently, so check back often to see what is new. There are also add-on video subscriptions available.

Prime Music

There are more than a million songs available to stream on compatible devices if you are an Amazon Prime member. This service is ad-free and available to those located within the United States and Puerto Rico. Playlists created by Amazon are available and you have the option of custom making your own. You can even incorporate tracks you have own your own computer.

Books

There are several advantages with your Amazon Prime membership involving downloading books. The Kindle Owner's Lending Library will be covered in detail in a later chapter. Members in the U.S. can also download one new book free per month earlier than non-members!

Shopping

In addition to the great shipping options, Amazon Prime opens up new options for what you can shop for and how. Whether you are shopping for electronics, clothes, birthday or Christmas gifts, or just stocking your pantry, Amazon has some exciting options for you. All the ways Amazon Prime can make shopping more fun and convenient will be covered later.

Prime Photos

Unlimited photo storage in the Amazon Cloud Drive is a major bonus of being a member. You will also receive 5 GB of storage for videos and documents. Photos are stored securely and can be backed up automatically if you choose. You can access your photos from anywhere. If photo storage is an issue for you, a Prime membership is actually cheaper than many external hard drives. If you do not renew or decide to cancel your membership, you will lose unlimited storage space and your photos will count towards your Amazon Drive storage limit.

The Rules

- Two-day shipping is not available on all items. Products not available under 2-day shipping will receive free standard shipping. These products generally have special shipping requirements.

- Amazon Prime is not intended for those who aim to resale their purchases made through Amazon.

- In some states, a sales tax will apply to your Amazon Prime Membership.

- Each specific feature of Amazon Prime will have its own rules and regulations specific to it.

Chapter 3: Membership Types and Sharing

Amazon Prime is the main and most common type of membership, and its benefits are what were discussed in the last chapter. You can either pay $99 for an entire year or pay $10.99 a month with the first month being considered a free trial either way. There are two variations of Prime memberships.

The first is Prime Student. In order to qualify for this type of membership, you will need to be currently enrolled in a college or university and have a valid .edu email address. With the student membership, there is no cost for the first six months but you do not get all of the benefits of a standard membership. You will still get the free 2-day shipping and access to thousands of streaming television shows and movies. If after six months you keep your account, you will be billed half the price of a non-student membership and get access to the full range of benefits.

There is also a Prime membership aimed at people only interested in video streaming. Prime Video memberships allow you to stream all of the videos available for Prime members. It costs $8.99 a month, with no yearly-pay option. It does not come with any of the other benefits of a Prime membership, and it does not include any additional subscriptions, which you can still add.

Additionally, it is possible to get an Amazon Prime trial membership to see if using this service is right for you. When signing up for Prime, click *Start Your 30-Day Free Trial*. If you do not already have an Amazon account, you will be asked to make one now. You will need to enter credit card information in order to get the trial. It is important to note that if you do not cancel after the 30-day period, you will be charged $99 for the year.

If you decide to cancel after the trial, log onto your account and click Settings. Then you will look for Manage Prime Account. On the left-hand side, there will be information on your trial account, including which day you will be charged for the year. Underneath this you can click *Do Not Continue*. You will be asked to confirm this. After clicking this, all Prime benefits will stop unless you decide to buy a membership.

Membership Sharing

It is possible for up to two adults and four children to share one Amazon Prime membership. In order to do this, you must create an Amazon Household. Both adults need to be present to set this up. You are able to link two separate Amazon accounts. Once both people are on the account, they can share many of the benefits of Amazon Prime as well as share content through a Family Library. You can share books, games, and apps this way.

Creating a household allows you to make profiles for your children and control the content they are viewing. Details on how to set

Parental Controls for what your child can view can be found in the Prime Video chapter.

Kindle Freetime Unlimited

Another way to control what your child is viewing on Amazon when sharing your Prime account is to subscribe to Kindle Freetime Unlimited. This service does cost extra, but you receive a considerable discount when you are an Amazon Prime Member. For one child, you will pay $2.99 a month instead of the $4.99 a month non-members pay. If you have more than one child, $6.99 allows you to have up to 4 child accounts, which beats the $9.99 non-members pay. This service is available on Kindle tablets, TVs, and Kindle readers.

In addition to blocking certain content, you can use this service to set educational goals and time limits. You can set it up so that your child cannot play games until their educational goals have been met for the day as well as let it know when bed time is so that it shuts itself off. Kids do not have access to the internet or social media while using FreeTime and they cannot make in-app purchases. It is a kid-friendly browsing environment that is ideal for children aged 3-12. Perhaps most importantly, kids cannot exit FreeTime without a password.

Giving Prime as a Gift

You can give the gift of a year of Amazon Prime to someone. In order to do this, provide Amazon with the gift recipient's email address and when you would like them to receive their gift. On this day, they will receive an email informing them of your gift and giving them instructions on how to activate their membership. They can begin their membership right away. If they are already a member of Amazon Prime, they can exchange it for an Amazon.com gift card. The membership will not automatically renew after a year. Only a yearly membership is available for giving as a gift, and only the full Prime membership is an option.

If you happen to live in or plan to visit the Seattle area, there is a physical location for Amazon Books. You can purchase a Prime Card to give as a gift, which is redeemable for a full year of Prime membership.

Chapter 4: Reading with Prime

The Kindle Owners' Lending Library

One of the biggest perks when becoming an Amazon Prime member is the ability to check out one new book every month completely free. The Kindle Owners' Lending Library (KOLL) includes thousands of books, including over one hundred New York Times best sellers. Borrowed books can be kept as long as you want but you may only have one out at a time. They can be read on Kindle e-readers as well as Kindle Fires and Fire phones as long as the device is registered to the account with the Prime membership. You can read your book on multiple devices as long as they are all linked to the same account. KOLL books cannot be read on the Kindle reading app.

To Borrow a Book

1. Open the Kindle Store on your compatible device.

2. Find the Kindle Owners' Lending Library on your device.

   a. On Kindle Fire tablets, select KOLL. On certain devices, you may need to swipe to the left in the Kindle Store to find KOLL.

   b. One Fire phones, swipe from the left inside the Kindle Store and then select *Kindle Lending Library*.

c. For Kindle e-readers, select either *All Categories* or *Menu* and find KOLL.

3. Chose a book. Eligible titles will have the Prime Badge underneath them.

4. Check out your book by hitting "Borrow for Free." If you still have last month's book, you will be prompted to return it at this time.

Please remember that if you cancel your membership or chose not to renew and have a borrowed KOLL book it will be automatically returned.

To Return a Book

1. Click on *Manage Your Devices and Content* and find the *Content* Tab.

2. Locate the book you would like to return and click the *Action* tab next to it.

3. Hit *Return This Book*. A dialogue box will come up asking if you are sure. Select yes.

Keep in mind there are no due dates. Any highlighting, bookmarking, or notes you have done will also be saved to your Amazon account, so if you decide to check out or buy the book in the future, you will still have them.

Kindle First

Do you like to be on top of the newest trends and hottest new book titles? If that is the case, Kindle First may make an Amazon Prime membership worth it all by itself. Each month, Amazon editors select six new books that are not available yet. As a Prime member, you are entitled to select one of these books to read absolutely free each month, before their official release date. The books change each month and each month you are able to select a new book.

Kindle Unlimited

Kindle Unlimited IS NOT part of your Amazon Prime membership, but something you can subscribe to supplement it. If you are an avid reader and decide that you need more than two books a month (one from the KOLL and one through Kindle First,) you can subscribe to Kindle Unlimited. As the title implies, you can download an unlimited number of books that in are in the Kindle Unlimited library. Keep in mind that large publishers generally do not allow their books to be included in this library and most books you can get using this service are at or below the $4.99 price point. Depending on what you read and how much you read, this may or may not be a useful addition to your Prime membership for you. It costs $9.99/month.

Borrowing Public Library Books

If you want the ability to read more books without paying extra, you can look into borrowing books from your local library. This is available to everyone, not just Amazon Prime members. More than 11,000 libraries across the United States have partnered with Amazon to provide free book check-outs for Kindle. You must be a member of the library you are trying to check a book out from. Using the specific library's website, you can check out Kindle books and have them sent to your Kindle Fire, Kindle e-reader, or your Kindle reading app. You will need to be connected to Wi-Fi while the library sends the book. The service that offers this is called OverDrive. Which books are available, and the length you can keep them out will vary by library. When it is time for the book to go back, Amazon will send you an email 3 days before it is due. You will also receive an email when the loan period is up, and the book has been returned. It is always possible to return a book before the loan period is up.

Chapter 5: Prime Instant Video

Streaming and downloading video is another big reason people get an Amazon Prime membership. Prime Video is only available to customers located in the United States and its territories due to licensing agreements. The videos are available to watch on any compatible device through Amazon Video. Amazon Video can be used on your computer as well as the following devices: Fire phones, Fire sticks, smart TVs, Amazon Fire TVs, Blu-ray players, video game consoles (Wii, Playstation, Xbox,) Android and iOS devices (in the form of an app,) and set-top boxes (Roku, TiVo, Google TV.)

When searching for something to watch, look for the category *Prime Video* or *Included with Prime*. All these titles are viewable with no extra charge. You can also filter search results to only include those titles included with Prime.

Need another reason to consider getting Amazon Prime? Amazon has exclusive content, not available for streaming or downloading anywhere else. They also offer original programming, with many children's, comedy, and drama titles currently available and titles from all genres in the works.

First Episode Free allows you to watch the first episode of select TV seasons at no charge. This feature is available to anyone with an Amazon account, however non-Prime members will have to sit through ad-breaks. To find eligible TV shows, open Amazon Video and find the *First Episode Free* category from either the *TV* or *Video* option.

Video quality will come at 4 different levels. They are Standard Definition (SD,) High Definition (HD,) and Ultra-High Definition (UHD.) What you are trying to watch and what device you are watching it on will affect which viewing options are available for you. If Ultra-High Definition is not good enough, some titles are being released in High Dynamic Range (HDR.) You can only view titles in HDR if you are using the Amazon App on certain models of Samsung or Sony TVs.

Creating a Watchlist

Overwhelmed by all the titles you can now access? You can create a Watchlist so you can access the shows and movies you want to watch in the future in one convenient place. This list is linked to both your account and your Amazon Video devices. When accessing it from the web, you can find *Your Watchlist* under *Your Account*. While browsing titles, you can simply click Add to Watchlist for things you think you will want to watch in the future. Already watched it or change your mind? Simply hit Remove from Watchlist under the video details.

Offline Viewing

Downloading certain titles to compatible devices is another option with membership. This is only available to the primary account holder; Household members receiving shared benefits are only eligible to stream video content. The devices that you can download content on are Kindle Fires that are newer than the 1st generation, Fire phones, and Android and iOS devices. Each download will only be available for a specified time. This length of time varies by title. You will receive a notification when your downloaded content is about to expire. Prime Video is only available to customers in the United States and its territories.

To Download a Title

1. Ensure your device is connected to Wi-Fi. It will need to maintain this connection for the duration of the download.
2. Select the Prime title you wish to download and look for video details.
3. Hit download. If you are trying to download an episode of a television show, select the episode and then select download.

With Amazon Prime Video, you can also use Amazon's X-Ray feature. Amazon has partnered with the Internet Movie Database (IMDb) to provide information of actors, background information, and much more. This feature is not available for every title. Look for the *X-Ray* label on the details page. The X-Ray feature is available while watching television shows or movies on your web browser, Android or iOS device, Fire tablet or TV, or Wii U. Whichever device you use, you will need to have access to Wi-Fi to use this feature.

Parental Controls

When using Amazon Video, especially when sharing with a household including young children, you may want to control what can be viewed and purchased. In order to do this, the first step is to set-up a 5-digit PIN. To set-up your PIN for the first time, access your account through your web browser or by using your Amazon Fire TV or TV stick. After doing so, you will need to enter this PIN before you can make a purchase through Amazon Video. This does not apply to Amazon Fire devices (TV, tablet, or phone) because these already have built-in parental controls.

You can use this same PIN to set viewing restrictions based on rating categories. You can customize what ratings you would like restricted and on which devices this should apply. Amazon bases their ratings on the MPAA rating classification system for movies and the TV Guidelines Organization TV Parental Guidelines for television shows. They combined these ratings into viewing levels with recommended audiences. These levels are General, Family, Teen, and Mature.

The Amazon Fire TV and Amazon Fire TV Stick will also use the 5-digit PIN you use for Amazon Video. With these, you can make changes directly on your device. Open *Settings* from your Fire TV and select the *Parental Controls* option. From here you can turn these controls on or off. It will ask you to enter your PIN or to set one up if you have not done so already. You can now block certain content and set viewing restrictions. You can also require the PIN to be entered to make any purchase, both digital and physical content.

There is a wide variety of controls you can set on your Amazon Fire Phone. To access them, go to *Settings*, *Applications*, and *Parental Controls*, then tap *Enable Parental Controls*. In addition to setting restrictions for video viewing, you can restrict social networking sharing, the camera, web browsing, internet access, and an assortment of other things.

The ability to restrict content on Kindle tablets depends on your type and generation. Once you have linked your tablet to your Amazon account, you can get personalized instructions for your specific device through their website.

Chapter 6: Prime Music

Amazon Prime members have access to millions of song titles. You can listen to music ad-free while enjoying unlimited skips. You can personalize a station based on your own music tastes. The list of songs available is always changing and worth checking often. You can also incorporate your own music from other sources into Amazon playlists.

The devices you can access Prime music on are as follows: Fire phones and tablets, the Amazon Fire TV, iOS and Android smartphones, Amazon Echo, the Fire TV stick, your PC or Mac, HEOS devices, Sonos devices, Play-Fi devices, and Bose SoundTouch systems.

The preferred format of music on Amazon in the Digital Music Store is MP3. Typically, a 3-minute songs will take up approximately 5MB of space. Amazon also supports non-DMR files in .mp3 and .m4a for playback, streaming, and downloading. Eligible files formatted in .wav, .wma, .ogg, .aiff, and .flac files can be imported if Amazon has the rights to the track in their Digital Music Store.

If you have the downloaded Amazon Music app on your phone or tablet, you can download Prime music for offline enjoyment. This music is only available through the app and cannot be transferred to other devices. Once you have downloaded the music, switch from your *Cloud Library* to your *Offline Library*.

You can add music you own from other sources to your Amazon Music library. Go to *Your Music Library* from your web browser on the computer that contains the music you would like to add. *Upload Your Music* will be an option on the left-hand side. If you have not already, you will be prompted to download Amazon Music. Follow the instructions on-screen. If you already have Amazon Music, you can skip the last two steps and open it directly. *Under Your Library* select *Upload*. From here, you can drag and drop files into your music library. Once you have done this, you can access this music from all of your connected Amazon Music devices. Add it to playlists to really customize your music experience.

While using Amazon Music, you can often view the song lyrics for the track you are listening to. This feature is available on Amazon Fire TVs and Tablets (except for the first generation Kindle Fire) and the Amazon App on Android and iOS devices. It can also be used through your web browser on either a PC or Mac. If the song you are listening to has lyrics available, a Lyrics badge will appear next to the song title. On the Now Playing screen you will also see either *Lyrics* or *X-Ray* as an option. While listening to a song, lyrics will display line-by-line and in time with the playback in the lyrics panel. This feature can be expanded to full screen or closed completely. If you are using a Kindle Fire Tablet, you can press and hold a song to view its lyrics even if the song is not currently playing. Lyrics are available through songs you are streaming as well as for songs you have purchased through the Digital Music Store. You can match songs that you import to the Digital Music Store and view their lyrics as well. If the song was transferred using USB or is not currently in the Digital Music Store the song lyrics will be unavailable.

Some things to keep in mind about Amazon Prime Music are that it is only available to the primary account holder, not additional Household members, and that you must have a United States billing address. You must also have an Amazon account linked to a valid U.S. bank. This service is not available to those using the Amazon Prime Student membership during their trial period.

Chapter 7: Shopping with Prime

Amazon 1-Click

Amazon 1-Click allows you to skip the shopping cart and place orders with one click of a button. It is set-up automatically the first time you make a purchase on Amazon. The method of payment and shipping address used for this first order will become your defaults for 1-Click shopping. It is important to keep this information up to date. Once you place an order, you have approximately 30 minutes to update your order information. You may turn off this option if you wish.

Amazon Prime Pantry

Prime Pantry is a service available exclusively to members, allowing you to purchase household goods at low prices and have them shipped at the low price of $5.99 per box. You can fit as much as possible in this box, which has a weight limit of 45 pounds and a size limit of 4 cubic feet. You do not need to fill the box completely to make your order. Be sure to check out their weekly deals and exclusive coupons you qualify for by being a Prime member.

This service is aimed at people trying to restock their nonperishable household products. Some examples of things you may buy through this service are diapers, cans of soda pop, cat litter, canned foods, and pet food. Having it delivered to your door for a low, flat rate can be much more convenient than a trip to the local bulk or grocery store. You can purchase both bulk and regular sized products through this service, adding to its appeal.

Exclusive Prime Coupons

There are many coupons available to Prime members exclusively. They are available for Grocery, Beauty Products, Health and Personal Care, School and Office Supplies, Automotive, and many other categories. On the coupon page, you will also see offers for Subscribe and Save. If you order subscriptions, you will receive a discount on Amazon or Amazon Marketplace items you have subscribed for, and they will arrive on the same day every month. Shipping for this service is free. You are not obligated to continue this service for any length of time and can cancel penalty free whenever suits you. You also have the option to skip a delivery if you are not ready for the next shipment. If you see a coupon you like, click *Clip Coupon* underneath the item, and the discount will be automatically applied at checkout.

Amazon Dash Button

An Amazon Dash Button allows the member to purchase buttons for popular products that you can then sync to your smartphone. Running out of an everyday item? Reordering can be as simple as pushing a button.

Once you receive the button or buttons you will be using; they must be linked to your Amazon account. Download the Amazon Shopping App from the Apple App Store or Google Play Store. Turn on both Wi-Fi and Bluetooth on your smartphone. Some buttons do not use Bluetooth and will simply use the Wi-Fi and your phone's speakers to communicate. The next step is to open the Amazon Shopping App, select *Menu, Your Account, My Dash Devices*, and then *Set-Up a New Device.* Sign in to your account and select *Accept and Get Started.* It is now time to hold down your Dash Button until the blue LED light flashes. In the app on your phone, hit Connect. You will then be prompted to enter your Wi-Fi network password. You can check the box to save the password, so you do not need to do this step every time.

Once the button is communicating with your phone, you will need to select exactly what product you want to be ordered when you click the button. This is where you can specify sizes and other variables. For example, if you are re-ordering your laundry detergent, which scent do you want? You will do this through the app on your phone. Finally, you will be asked to confirm your 1-click shipping and payment information. This is the info that will be used when you place an order. The final step is to find a convenient spot to stick the button. The button should be placed on a plastic or metal surface that has been cleaned in advance. In order to stick-on, remove the backing and hold down firmly for 10 seconds. To remove, slowly peel off. The best place for your button is a flat wall or another vertical surface.

Worried about accidental orders? When the button is pressed, Amazon will send a confirmation notice to your phone. At this time, you can easily cancel the order if you change your mind or it was unintentional. Unless you change this option, the Dash Button Order Protection will not allow a new order to be placed until the last order has been shipped.

Amazon Elements

The products available through Amazon Elements are designed to put the customer at ease because you know exactly what you are getting. They vow to listen to the feedback of the consumer when making all decisions regarding these products such as packaging design. They will only use top of the line ingredients and things they are comfortable using with their own family. Being up-front about what you are buying, what is in the product, and how it is made is another way they hope to set you at ease. These products are available exclusively to Amazon Prime members.

Every Amazon Elements product comes with a code. This code can be scanned using your phone and the latest version of the Amazon App. While it looks similar, it is not a QR code, and you should not try to scan it using a QR scanner. Peel off the top layer of the sticker and point your phone's camera at it to scan. The information that will pop-up includes when and where the product was made, its best-by date, when it was ordered, when it was delivered, the origin of each ingredient, the purpose of each ingredient, the story behind the suppliers, and other information specific to the product you have ordered. It also gives you the opportunity to leave feedback and rate the product. Additionally, you can re-order the product using this code. If the sticker is missing, has been peeled off already, or is damaged in a way that prevents it from being scanned, Amazon cannot the origin and will either refund or replace your item.

Completion Discount

Amazon Prime can also help a family get ready for the arrival of a little one with 10-15% off of your online baby registry. Your registry will need to be at least 14 days old before you are eligible for this discount. You also need to be within 60 days of your due date. When you have met the eligibility requirements, a message will appear on the top of your registry letting you know. The discount is good for an order up to 5000 US dollars, which will save you $750. You may use this discount one time only, up to 180 days after your due date.

To create your registry, click *Wish List* on the top of any Amazon.com page. Select *Baby Registry* from the drop-down menu that appears, then click *Create*. The on-screen instructions will walk you through the process of creating your new registry. You can edit your name and email address in the *About You section*. You can also add a Co-Registrant so that people can search for the registry using your partner's name. You can now search the

Baby Store and other product categories and add things to your registry by clicking on Add to Baby Registry, located under the Buy button on the product's description page. You cannot add items that are currently out of stock to the registry.

Another baby-friendly benefit that Amazon offers is the diaper subscriptions, which can save you up to 20% and a trip to the store with a newborn.

Prime Now

Believe it or not, Prime customers in certain geographical areas can order items and food from restaurants and receive them in as little as an hour. This is a service available exclusively to Prime members, and it is available from 6 a.m. to midnight, 7 days a week. If you can wait two hours, the delivery is free. If you need it in an hour, the charge is $7.99. There are tens of thousands of items available through this service, with more being added all of the time. When ordering from a restaurant, download the Prime Now app. If you live in an area that offers the service, you will see a selection of restaurants to choose from. Once your order is placed, both the restaurant and delivery person are immediately notified. Amazon will then pick up the order and pack it in an insulated container and bring it to you. This should be done within the hour, with the average time being around 39 minutes.

Prime Day

This is a 1-day-only sale available exclusively to Amazon Prime members. Items go on sale from almost every product category, with some of the biggest discounts Amazon ever offers. These deals are comparable to prices you would find on Black Friday and happens once a year!

Video Game Discount

Are you or someone you love a big gamer? Amazon Prime members get 20% off pre-order and new release video games. This only applies to physical games (not digital downloads) that are shipped and sold by Amazon.   If you order during a game's pre-order period or within two weeks of its release, your 20% off discount will be automatically applied at checkout.

Lightning Deals and Prime Early Access

Special daily deals, called Lightning Deals, have a limited quantity available at a special discounted price. Anyone can shop for Lightning Deals, but certain deals have Prime Early Access which allows you to start shopping 30 minutes sooner than the general public. Being a Prime member does not ensure you will get the deal as they are all "while supplies last" and some deals will sell out during the early access period. In addition to being limited in quantity available, Lightning Deals are only available for a short period of time. You can browse future deals and place a

Watch on upcoming deals to make sure you do not miss it. You will receive a notification on your phone if you have the latest version of the Amazon App and have notifications turned on.

Amazon Fresh

Amazon Fresh IS NOT included with Prime membership. However, Prime members can get a 90-day free trial of this service. The service is designed to offer early morning or next day delivery of fresh grocery products as well as things available to you locally. Currently, only people living in Seattle, New York, or certain parts of California can use this service. Amazon hopes to expand it in the near future. If you decide you like the service after your 90-day trial period, it will cost you $299 a year to have both the Prime and Prime Fresh membership.

For such a steep price, what do you get? Amazon promises a high level of quality in the items you are receiving, and takes extra care to keep things at their proper temperatures. There are two options for when you receive your Fresh delivery. The first, and more popular, is Doorstep Delivery. With this option, you select a 3-hour window in which the package can be delivered. You do not have to be home to receive the package, and it will come in a temperature-controlled tote bag. The bags are designed to keep your food fresh for up to one hour after the end of your delivery window. The totes are filled with frozen water bottles to keep your food cold. These water bottles are safe to drink and do not need to be returned to Amazon. These tote-bags are collected when the driver drops off your next delivery. In order to qualify for Doorstep Delivery, the driver must have unobstructed access to your doorstep. The other option you can choose is Attended Delivery. For this, you select a 1-hour window in which you promise to be home to receive your order. This is the option you will need to use if you live in a secure building. Another perk is you do not need to store their temperature-controlled tote bags in your home.

On top of paying to be a member, you will need to pay $7.99 for shipping if your order total is less than $35. Orders above that ship for free. Also, you will be required to cover the cost of the groceries you have ordered. Get your order in before 10 a.m. if you want to receive it the same day. Additionally, if you do not wish to continue with Amazon Fresh after the trial period, it is up to you to cancel, or you will be automatically billed. The cost of the membership is pricey, but the items you buy can be significantly cheaper than you would find in stores so it may work out in your favor financially in the long run if you use the service a lot.

Chapter 8: Quick FAQs

- How much does it cost to join Amazon Prime?
  - A yearly membership costs $99, or you can pay $10.99 a month. A video-only membership is available at $8.99 a month. College students qualify for six months free and then a yearly membership at $49.
- How do you sign up for Amazon Prime?
  - Memberships can be purchased on Amazon.com. You will need an Amazon account and a valid credit card.
- Can you try Amazon Prime for free before buying?
  - A free trial of Amazon Prime is available if you have a valid credit card and Amazon account. Be sure to cancel before the 30-day trial period expires if you do not wish to be a member.
- How do I cancel my free trial?
  - Log into your account, click on *Manage Prime Membership* and click *Do Not Continue*.
- How do I cancel Amazon Prime if I am not in my free-trial period?
  - Log into your account, click on *Manage Prime Membership*, and select *End Membership*.
- What areas offer same-day shipping?

- This is available in Seattle/Tacoma, Los Angeles, the San Francisco area, San Diego, Fort Worth/Dallas, Phoenix, Indianapolis, New York City, Chicago, Baltimore, Atlanta, Tampa Bay, Washington DC, Orlando, Philadelphia, and Boston. Amazon hopes to continue expanding this service.
  - What areas offer Prime Now Restaurant delivery?
    - This service is currently available in Seattle, Dallas, Los Angeles, San Francisco, Atlanta, Austin, Miami, Baltimore, and Portland, OR. Amazon is expanding this service to other areas.
  - Do I get exclusive access to certain items?
    - Yes! On top of being able to shop Amazon's Element line, they occasionally offer items exclusively to Prime members.
  - What is an Amazon Household?
    - Amazon Households are created to share digital content and certain Prime benefits with other members of your family. You can add two adults, each with a separate Amazon account, and up to four children to your Amazon Household.
  - What benefits can be shared with members of my Amazon Household?

- The benefits that can be shared are as follows: Streaming Prime Video, the fast and free Prime shipping options, early access to Amazon Lightning Deals, the benefits of Prime Photos (each adult has their own unlimited account and will not share actual photos or albums,) use of the Kindle Owners' Lending Library, the 20% off diaper subscription discount, and the 15% discount on their baby registry.
- What is Prime Day?
  - Prime Day is a member-only sales event, where Amazon promises discounts and deals to rival the ones usually reserved for Black Friday, all from the comfort of your own home.
- Where can I watch Amazon Prime Videos?
  - Almost any device is now compatible with Amazon Prime. You can watch on PCs, Macs, the newest generations of all gaming systems, Kindle tablets, as well as many Smart TVs and smartphones. Unless you previously downloaded the title, you will need internet access.
- Is will being a Prime member give me access to all of Amazon Video's titles for free?
  - No, it will not. Not all titles are available under Prime and those

that are not will need to be purchased separately.

- o Do I need to be online to access Prime Video and Music?
    - For the most part, Amazon Music and Amazon Video are streaming services. However, as a Prime member, you can download certain titles so that you can enjoy them even if your device is offline.
- o What items generally qualify for 2-day shipping?
    - Almost all items sold by Amazon will qualify. Larger items, like treadmills and other oversized items, may not. Those sold by third parties via the Amazon Marketplace may not; it is up to the individual seller.
- o Does Amazon offer a referral credit for people who get family and friends to sign up?
    - Yes, they do. If the person you refer is a first-time Prime member, you will receive a $10 credit the first time an order they placed after becoming a memberships. If the person recently had a free-trial, they may not qualify to earn you the referral credit. This credit is not available to people living in Arkansas, Colorado, Maine, Missouri, Rhode Island, and

Vermont due to restrictions in those states.

- There is also a credit for referring someone to a Student Prime membership. This credit is for $5, and there is no purchase necessary to receive your credit. Both you and your friend will receive the credit, though it may take up to 7 days to show up in your account.

- Does Amazon Prime come with Kindle Freetime Unlimited?
  - No, it does not. It is an optional addition that you can purchase for a discount if you are a Prime member.

Conclusion

Thank you again for downloading this book!

I hope this book was able to help you to make the very most out of your Amazon Prime membership.

The next step is to start using Amazon to do the things you love, whether it be listening to music, reading a good book, watching the latest television shows and movies, storing your photos, or doing some online shopping. Simplify your life with fast and free shipping on everyday products and easy product ordering.

Finally, if you enjoyed this book, please take the time to share your thoughts and post a review on Amazon. It'd be greatly appreciated!

Thank you and good luck!

E-book Description

Did you recently decide to become an Amazon Prime member? Are you debating whether it is right for you? This book will detail all the advantages of signing up, as well as the expenses and how to get the most out of your membership.

Not sure how to stream or download video? How about stream music and play music on multiple devices? Want to the ability to re-order groceries with the click of an actual button? Do you like reading the latest book before your friends and family? Do you spend a lot of time shopping online and want your items faster? This book will teach you how to do all of these things, plus detail the other lesser-known advantages of becoming an Amazon Prime member.

5 Reasons You Need this Book to Fully Enjoy Amazon Prime:

1. Detailed instructions on how to import your own music into your Amazon Music library
2. Tips on making the most out of your movie and TV watching experience, including what video quality is available and how to learn about the title while watching it
3. Detailed instructions on how to set-up Parental Controls so that you know exactly what content your child is viewing through Prime

4. A thorough explanation of the Kindle Owners' Lending Library and how to take advantage of it
5. Instructions on how to set up your Amazon Household and share some Prime benefits with the members of your family

Added Benefits of Reading Amazon Prime: How to Make the Most Out of the Many Benefits of Amazon Prime:

- Information on Prime Day, Amazon's own Black Friday type sale

- Learn how new moms and their families can save big with Prime

- Discover what Prime Pantry is and how it can simplify your life

- Tips on how to save money and get the biggest discounts

11260138R00026

Made in the USA
Lexington, KY
08 October 2018